Foreword

The Rosary has
prayer life for ce
generation have
the simplicity o:
prayers, repeate
actions towards God. At the same time,
through meditation, God's presence is
discovered in the depth of each mystery.

The meditations in this booklet are
offered as a fresh approach to help us
enter into the Rosary mysteries. From the
Annunciation, where heaven meets Mary
on earth, the meditations journey through
the birth, life, ministry, passion, death and
resurrection of Jesus, to that destination
moment where Mary is crowned Queen of
Heaven.

How to pray the Rosary with this booklet
As we progress in praying the Rosary,
each of us will find our own unique and
individual way to combine both elements
of prayers and meditations. As an initial
guide, each decade of the Rosary has

a specific meditation which can be read through slowly and thoughtfully before reciting the prayers. Allow for words, images or thoughts from the meditation to come to mind as the decade prayers are being said. This can be difficult at first and will require some practice. Rosary mysteries are just that, mysteries. We will never exhaust any of the Rosary mysteries in our lifetime of praying and journeying. A variation may include breaking each meditation into smaller sentences and reading these between one or more Hail Marys as the decade is recited. Given the breadth of the meditations, their use can extend beyond the Rosary setting to help reflection and discussion in parishes, schools and homes, which in turn could help in renewed energy for the Rosary.

Kieran Hill

Meditations on the Rosary

Kieran Hill is a qualified social worker. He has been involved in Church liturgy for many years, and more recently found himself drawn to the Rosary and the mysteries contained within. This is his first book.

Meditations on the Rosary

Kieran Hill

Published 2012 by Veritas Publications
7–8 Lower Abbey Street
Dublin 1, Ireland
publications@veritas.ie
www.veritas.ie

ISBN 978 1 84730 394 3

Designed by Heather Costello, Veritas Publications
Printed by Nicholson & Bass Ltd, Newtownabbey

Veritas books are printed on paper made from the wood pulp of
managed forests. For every tree felled, at least one tree is planted,
thereby renewing natural resources.

Contents

Prayer Before the Rosary

Queen of the Holy Rosary, you have deigned to come to Fatima to reveal to the three Shepherd children the treasures of grace hidden in the Rosary. Inspire my heart with a sincere love of this devotion, in order that by meditating on the Mysteries of our Redemption which are recalled in it, I may be enriched with its fruits and obtain peace for the world, the conversion of sinners, and the favour which I ask of you in this Rosary. (*Here mention your request.*) I ask it for the greater glory of God, for your own honour, and for the good of souls, especially for my own. Amen.

Prayers of the Rosary

The Apostles' Creed

I believe in God,
the Father almighty,
Creator of heaven and earth,
and in Jesus Christ, his only Son, our Lord,

who was conceived by the Holy Spirit,
born of the Virgin Mary,
suffered under Pontius Pilate,
was crucified, died and was buried;
he descended into hell;
on the third day he rose again from the dead;
he ascended into heaven,
and is seated at the right hand of God
the Father almighty;
from there he will come to judge the living
and the dead.

I believe in the Holy Spirit,
the holy catholic Church,
the communion of saints,
the forgiveness of sins,
the resurrection of the body,
and life everlasting. Amen.

The Our Father

Our Father, who art in heaven,
hallowed be thy name.
Thy kingdom come.
Thy will be done, on earth as it is in heaven.
Give us this day our daily bread.
And forgive us our trespasses,
as we forgive those who trespass against us.
And lead us not into temptation,
but deliver us from evil. Amen.

The Hail Mary

Hail Mary,
full of Grace,
the Lord is with thee.
Blessed art thou among women,
and blessed is the fruit of thy womb, Jesus.
Holy Mary,
mother of God,
pray for us sinners now,
and at the hour of death. Amen.

Glory be to the Father

Glory be to the Father, and to the Son, and to the Holy Spirit. As it was in the beginning, is now, and ever shall be, world without end. Amen.

Fatima Prayer

O my Jesus, forgive us our sins, save us from the fires of hell, lead all souls to heaven, especially those in most need of thy mercy. Amen.

The Joyful Mysteries

The Joyful Mysteries are said on:
Mondays
Saturdays
Sundays of Advent
Sundays from Epiphany until Lent

1. The Annunciation
2. The Visitation
3. The Nativity
4. The Presentation of Jesus at the Temple
5. The Finding of the Child Jesus in the Temple

1. The Annunciation

An angel, eternally standing in the presence
of God,
returns to earth to stand in the presence of
God's favoured one, Mary.

A soul, at conception infused to capacity
with grace and deep longing, now stirred to
respond to the Angel's greeting
'Full of grace'.

Grace connects with grace.
Longing connects with longing.
Heaven connects with earth.

Mary's undoubting acceptance of God's will
joyfully echoing –

Salvation is Conceived.

2. The Visitation

Two kinswomen embrace in celebration of
new life conceived.
Earthly impossibilities overwhelmed in a
spring of spiritual supremacy.

Angelic annunciations confirmed in glance,
touch, voice and soul.

Kin connects with Kin.
Womb connects with Womb.
Spirit connects with Spirit.

Elizabeth, ignited by Joy,
Spirit sourced,
shouts to the world that
Mary is the Mother of God.

Salvation is Exclaimed.

3. The Nativity

Joseph, called by Caesar to Census,
Mary, called by God to Confinement,
Journey together to the City of David.

Centuries of prophecy and promise awaiting
fulfilment as Heaven journeys to Earth.

Divine descent complete,
the King of kings is earthed, through Mary, in
total humility.
Nothing to distract focus, in wonderment,
they gaze at God made Child.

Angelic choirs alone sing Glory, sounding to
the shepherds and world that

   Salvation is Born.

4. The Presentation of Jesus at the Temple

Faithful to the Law, Jesus is carried to the Temple.
Presented as first-born, the Christ Child is declared Holy as exchange offerings are made.
Redemption for the Redeemer ritually bestowed.
Purity to Mary, never lost, ritually restored.

Simeon, spiritually sensitive, approaches and takes hold of God's Promise in a praise-filled moment.

Old connects with New.
Light connects with Light.
Simeon sings that

Salvation is Seen.

5. The Finding of the Child Jesus in the Temple

Unknowingly, each step taken by Mary and Joseph towards Nazareth takes them further away from Jesus.

They rendezvous in the realisation that the 'Divine Treasure' entrusted to their care is lost.
   They search.
   Three days.

Eyes opened in astonishment, find the Source of all knowledge asking questions of the Temple teachers.

Mary maternally seeks meaning.
Jesus provides Paternal purpose –
   Father's House.
   Father's Work.

Mary quietly remembers.

   Salvation is found.

The Mysteries of Light

The Mysteries of Light are said on:
Thursdays

1. The Baptism of Jesus
2. The Wedding at Cana
3. Jesus' Proclamation of the Kingdom of God
4. The Transfiguration
5. The Institution of the Eucharist

1. The Baptism of Jesus

A prophet preaches repentance.
Streams of sinners flood Jordan's banks to
confess and be baptised.

Jesus, from Nazareth, stands in solidarity
with the expectant pilgrims who
    descend and emerge,
    descend and emerge,
    descend and emerge
to John's announcement and the cleansing
flow of the Jordan.

Kin connects again with Kin.
In open water, John looks at Jesus as he halts
his baptismal flow in recognition of a Higher
Power.
    Jesus explains –
    Obedience to God's Will.
    John resumes.

Jesus descends and emerges to his Father's
announcement of approval and the anointing
flow of the Holy Spirit, Dove-like.
Father, Son and Holy Spirit.

2. The Wedding at Cana

Cana celebrates a wedding.
Mary is invited to the feast.
Jesus attends along with his disciples.

Seeing need, Mary intercedes with her Son –
No wine.

Sensitive to the unspoken request and his
Father's will, Jesus replies –
    Not his hour.

Cana connects to Calvary.

Mary knows her son and
servants are told to do what Jesus tells.
Purification pots are filled to capacity.
Jesus transforms –
    Water into wine.
    Scarcity into abundance.
    Old into new.

Celebration cups replenished, the
new wine is best.
Disciples start to believe as Jesus' ministry is
manifest.

3. Jesus' Proclamation of the Kingdom of God

Baptist's work completed, the people still seek Israel's Saviour. Reputation spreading, large crowds gather wherever Jesus is proclaiming God's Kingdom –

> Synagogues
> Streets
> Shores.

Throughout Galilee and beyond, in word and deed, Jesus brings the Kingdom close and present.
Mercy and forgiveness to the repentant.
Healing to the sick.
God's supremacy and mercy manifest in miracles worked –

> Blind see.
> Deaf hear.
> Lame walk.
> Dignity restored.

Better is still to come as Jesus missions his disciples to proclaim God's Kingdom.

4. The Transfiguration

Jesus ascends a high mountain taking those
close and chosen, Peter, James and John, with
him.

In prayer with the Father, Jesus' appearance
alters, garments glow in luminous white.
Light connects with Light.
Son connects with Father.

Drowsiness diminished, senses shocked, the
Apostles glimpse Divinity and past prophets,
Moses and Elijah, conversing –
    Salvations' journey to
    Jerusalem.

Old covenant connects with New.

To retain the presence Peter proposes three
tents.
A Father-filled cloud descends precipitating a
heavenly announcement –

    This is his Son.
    Listen to Him.

5. The Institution of the Eucharist

In Jerusalem, Peter and John prepare the Passover. Jesus gathers that evening to celebrate the meal.
In Love the Divine Master rises and, washing the feet of the Apostles, commands them to follow his example.

Taking bread, Jesus –
    Gives Thanks
    Says Blessing
    Breaks
    Shares
His Body.

Taking the Chalice –
    Gives Thanks
    Says Blessing
    Shares
His Blood.

New Covenant.
Forgiveness of sins.

Jesus Commands –

    Do in remembrance of him.

The
Sorrowful
Mysteries

The Sorrowful Mysteries are said on:
Tuesdays
Fridays
Daily from Ash Wednesday until Easter
Sunday

1. The Agony in the Garden
2. The Scourging at the Pillar
3. The Crowning with Thorns
4. The Carrying of the Cross
5. The Crucifixion

1. The Agony in the Garden

Jesus gathers as night falls on Gethsemane.
A distance apart, those close and chosen are
requested to watch and pray.
  Three times;
  Too much to watch.

Jesus falls to ground as Adam's fall is
confronted.
Chalice contents comprehended, in complete
abandonment to the Father's Will, Jesus prays
for suffering to pass;
perspiration in his pleading
falling to earth like drops of blood.

Gethsemane connects
with Eden
Love connects with Love.
Will connects with Will.

Angelic strength received, Jesus wakes the
weak and announces –

  Saviour is betrayed.

2. The Scourging at the Pillar

Pilate looks at Jesus.
Authorities, one heavenly, confront.
Questions unanswered,
no plea in defence offered, Jesus remains firm
to his Mission. In his silence, no guilt is found.

 The crowd are to decide –
    Jesus or Barabbas?
    Guiltless or guilty?

Three times asked,
the same returned –
    Release Barabbas.
    Crucify Jesus.

Jesus is scourged.
Wrongly whipped and painfully marked, he is
handed back to his accusers.

Pilate concedes –

    Saviour is sentenced to death.

3. The Crowning with Thorns

Jesus is taken into Pilate's palace.
His accusers cannot follow.
Hundreds of Roman soldiers gather as the
mockery commences.

Not befitting a 'king', Jesus' clothes are
stripped from him and replaced by a Roman
robe of red.

Still not enough kinglike, a crown of twisted
thorns thrusts downwards into his Head, a
reed sceptre sculpted in his right hand. Now,
on bended knee, they can hail Jesus as a 'king'.

Military mockery and humiliation striking
out with every blow and spit rained down
upon Jesus.

Mockery meets Meekness.
Falsehood meets Truth.
Insult meets Love.

4. The Carrying of the Cross

Jesus takes his first step under the weight of the cross. A large crowd joins the path to Golgotha, moving to the pace of Pilate's punishment.

Soldiers seize Simon
and compel him to carry the Cross.

Fused by force, Simon connects with Jesus. So close, Jesus fills his vision as footstep follows Holy footstep.

Women in mournful procession attract attention. Jesus responds to sorrow, both present and future.

Love, not force, moves Jesus on.
To finish his Journey,
to face his final sacrifice.

5. The Crucifixion

Jesus, again, is stripped of his clothes.
His hands and feet nailed to the Cross,
personalised by Pilate –
'King of the Jews'.

Centred between two others condemned,
mockery and insult continue. Jesus is
challenged, unknowingly, to reveal his Divine
Power and deny his Father's Will.

Love holds firm –
Paradise promised to the repentant.
Pardon petitioned for his abusers.

Mary stands at the foot of the Cross.
Jesus looks at his Mother and closest disciple
– a bond of care is sealed in sorrow foretold
by Simeon.

His sacrifice reaching its climax, last breath
spent, Jesus commends his Spirit to his
Father.

Death is confronted.

The Glorious Mysteries

The Glorious Mysteries are said on:
Wednesdays
Sundays from Easter until Advent

1. The Resurrection
2. The Ascension
3. The Descent of the Holy Spirit
4. The Assumption of Mary
5. The Coronation of the Virgin

1. The Resurrection

Sun rises on the third day and some women
journey to tend the body of Jesus. An angel,
luminous like lightening, shocks senses as –
  Earth shakes.
  Sentries swoon.
  Sepulchre's stone shifts.

Fear and joy combine as angelic annunciation
of resurrection explains the empty tomb –
  Jesus crucified.
  Jesus raised.
  Jesus going to Galilee.

Missioned to herald the news, the women
run back to the Apostles.
Disbelief suspended, Peter and John hasten
to the tomb.
Burial cloths alone remain within.
John believes –

  Saviour has Risen.

2. The Ascension

Forty days the Apostles and followers
witness Jesus raised from the dead.
Still bearing the wounds and stripes of
suffering, it is the same Jesus, but changed.

Now, not bound by human limitations, the
Risen Jesus appears and disappears from
their presence in new ways.
Jesus gathers his disciples at Bethany.

Arms raised in blessing, his humanity
begins its heavenly ascent, complete when
enthroned at his Father's right hand.
Full of resurrected joy, Jesus' followers fill the
temple with praise.

Saviour ascends to the Father.

3. The Descent of the Holy Spirit

Pentecost morning and the Apostles and
followers gather. Without warning, the house
resounds with a heaven-sent sound, like
a powerful wind. A promised presence is
announced.

The Holy Spirit, a burning flame, separates
and shapes like tongues of fire, descends
upon each Apostle.
Spirit connects with Spirit.
Tongues of men gifted and inflamed to
proclaim God's truth in other tongues.
Many nationalities amazed to hear, without
translation, about the resurrected Jesus.
Peter proclaiming to the listeners
and world –

Receive the Holy Spirit.

4. The Assumption of Mary

Mary is
  Full of grace.
  Free from sin.
  Blessed among women.
  New Eve.
  Mother of God.
Obedient to God's word, Mary shares in the
birth, life, passion, death and resurrection of
Jesus.
Sanctuary of the Word Incarnate,
Mary is granted favours beyond earthly life.
Her body preserves from decay into dust and
transcends her tomb.
In life Mary presents Jesus to others.
In death, nothing barring resurrection
reward, Jesus presents Mary, body and soul
unified, to his Father.

Earth connects with Heaven.
Mother connects with Son.
Death connects with Eternal Life.

5. The Coronation of the Virgin

Assumed to her Son, enthroned in his
Kingdom, Mary shares in Heavenly
Glorification –
Her whole being bathes in Perpetual Light as
she connects with Heavenly Royalty.

Beyond beatitudes, Pinnacle of perfection,
Mary is crowned
Queen of Heaven and Earth –
   Crown of stars
   Clothed with the sun
   Moon under her feet.

Always sourcing the Sacred,
Mary eternally presents her Son to Humanity.

   Mother of God.
   Our Lady.
   Our Mother.

Prays for all to reach their
Destination –

   Heaven.